WHAUP O' THE REDE

WHAUP O' THE REDE

A BALLAD OF THE BORDER RAIDERS

BY

WILL OGILVIE

DALBEATTIE: THOMAS FRASER

1909

Printed by
FRASER, ASHER & CO. LIMITED
164 Howard Street
Glasgow
For THOMAS FRASER, Dalbeattie

TO

WALTER SCOTT OF HARDEN

BARON POLWARTH

BY

PERMISSION

IS DEDICATED THIS

BALLAD OF THE RAIDERS

PREFACE

THE FOLLOWING is a simple and rugged song in simple words, dealing with the strenuous times of our forbears, and founded on a well-known incident in raiding warfare. It is written down from the fulness of a heart that loves every leaf and grass blade on the Borders, and it is written for those understanding people whose heritage is the memory and legend that wraps romance around the Marches. If it brings to them anything of the freshness of those glorious hills among which its scenes are laid, anything of the spirit of those stirring days in which our forefathers fought and rode, anything of the lights and shadows that roll unceasingly across the slopes of Cheviot and down the Ettrick valley, it has not been written in vain.

THE AUTHOR.

WHAUP O' THE REDE

INTRODUCTION

B

INTRODUCTION

ED ON the darkness the
streamers run
Of a flame that is not of the
rising sun,
And the shriek that echoes from hill to vale
Is more than the questing curlew's wail,
For the gate of a Border keep's in flame
And the ravens feast on its fallen fame.
There are cattle that rose ere the feeding hour,
There are women that weep on a wasted tower,
For, swift as the deer on Ettrick Pen
Sweep at a sound from scaur to glen,
And swift as the towering kestrel stoops
When a field mouse moves in the bracken hoops,

Ere dawn had silvered the misty Rede
Wat Harden had ridden to Ravensmead,
Had rapped with his pike on the rusty door
That had countered full many a charge before,
Had cried to the startled guard " To arms!
How fatten the kye on your Redeside farms?"
Then the court had filled with a martial clang
As over the stones the spurred heels rang,
And the Nevilles poured through the open door
To close with their ancient foes once more.
Ere the last pale star had died in the west,
Ere the sun had flooded the Carter crest,
The chief of the Nevilles lay dead in the fern
Where the fight had raged at the bend of the burn,
And a dozen henchmen lay stretched beside,
Who had scorned to live where their leader died.
   The ruthless raider reined his steed
On the crown of the March: behind him the Rede
Wound glittering down through the autumn flowers
And was lost in the smoke of the smouldering towers.

Then Wat, with a wave of his bridle hand:
" I have lit them a torch in Northumberland!
Full many a steer ha' they reft o' mine,
But aye they ha' paid me in kine for kine,
And this ye may take as Wat Harden's word:
Each stot they ha' stolen comes hame wi' a herd!
Now loose your girths for a breathing space
Ere the deep o' the moss to Jed we face,
And turn your steeds to the morning wind,
For yon brae was steep we ha' left behind;
The kye are weary o' mire and fern
And 'tis many a mile to the Kirkhope burn!"
  He spoke. Each rider loosed his gear.
Then sudden to Wat o' Harden's ear
Came a wailing note that the reiver knew
Was neither the scream of the grey sea-mew
Seeking the Solway, nor yet the cry
Of the restless whaup as it circled by.
Sternly he glanced where the loot o' the Rede
Was bound to the back of each reeking steed.

" Ho! Ralph!" he cried to a trooper tall
Whose load was the widest among them all,
Whose croup and cantle could scarce be seen
For a couch's spoil and its silken sheen:
" Is your nag not hauden enough wi' weight
That ye carry the care o' some moorcock's mate?
Are we callants nesting in wold or wood
That ye harry some late-hatched grey-hen's brood?"
Ralph Scott leapt up from the rustbrown heath
With a reckless Border oath in his teeth,
But he slid his hand the silks beneath;
Then he flushed to the brow as his fingers found—
A child!—in a soft white kirtle wound;
And he held it high to the bearded line:—
" 'Tis a nestling, laird; but no spoil of mine!"
Wat o' Harden laughed till the moss hags shook
And the stone-chat rose from the glidder neuk,
Then he took the babe in his rough right hand
Saying " Cry, little whaup, to Northumberland!

For thy sire lies dead in the trodden brake
And thy mother weeps for her warrior's sake,
And the smoke of thine home lies black on the
     cloud!
But turn to the Teviot; now, laugh loud!
For the sun is shining on bucht and bower
And I'll find thee a mother in Kirkhope Tower!"

The sun was setting on Kirkhope Swire,
The sky in the West was a field of fire,
The bee had flown from the bloom o' the ling,
The blackcock's head was over his wing,
The oaks in the forest stood stern and still
And the Ettrick whispered to Kirkhope Hill.
The Lady had tired of the watch she kept
And over her spinning had bowed and slept,
When a spurred heel clanked on the boarded floor
And a gauntlet smote on the darkened door,
And a henchman roared " Doth my lady ken
That the haugh is ringing wi' Harden's men?

The moon on their bridle bits doth shine

And whitens the horns of the English kine!"

The Lady rose from her idle wheel

And looked to the Ettrick, pleased and proud,

She heard the clang of the riders' steel,

The trampling hoofs and the laughter loud,

And " Open the door of the keep!" she cried,

"There is spoil when the lairds of Harden ride!"

The horses tossed to the peat-banks brown

A silver spray from the moonlit burn,

And the Lady sped like a spurwing down,

The first to welcome her lord's return;

And hand of the silk and hand of the sword

Were crossed as the roan horse crossed the ford.

" What have you there that you shield from harm

So close in the curve of your bridle arm?"

Then Walter of Harden leaned across;

He was splashed with the mire of the Carter moss,

His brow was blackened with sweat and smoke,

There was blood on his hand and his brand was

broke,

But he smiled on his lady and bowed full low
As he gave her the child from his saddle bow :—
" I have ridden the Marches, boy and man,
For more than the reiver's wonted span,
I have lifted horses and driven steers,
I have kindled the faggots for thirty years,
I have broken some crowns in my time, I trow,
But I never have warred upon babes—till now!
And this prize that was reft from a lady's bower
Shall be gift to the Lady of Kirkhope Tower!
Take him and keep him!" Wat Harden cried,
" Blood must be spilt when the raiders ride.
What peace would there be on the Border Line
If I left to the English their lifted kine?
As long as they ravish my Ettrick herds
So long shall I meet them with pikes—not words;
So long shall I raid on the Redeside lands
But—I hold no quarrel with swaddling bands,
And that boy should have slept in his mother's arm
    On the English side of the March to-night,

In a blackened tower on a wasted farm
  By the burning lintel's lurid light,
Had that rascal Ralph his spoil laid bare
Ere he bound it to burden my good grey mare!
But take him and keep him, this whaup o' the
        Rede,
For, by Michael! he comes of a full blooded breed,
And of all my brave foemen the bravest and best
Bore the raven of Neville engraved on his crest.
Take him and nurse him to manhood; then
He shall ride on the moss with the Harden men!"
He ceased, and the roan horse climbed the steep
And his red hoofs rang in the court of the keep.
The Lady looked up with a word of blame,
Then bent to the child with some soft love-name;
" For the sake of your sire in his long last sleep,
And your mother that many a night shall weep
For a stricken lord and a stolen son,
I shall do as your mother herself had done

Had they brought her a sweet-faced bairn of mine
As a gift of the raid with our Ettrick kine.
I shall nurse thee, bud of the English rose,
   Till thou growest great as my lord in war,
But of mercy more than my lord bestows
   On the widowed wife and the bairn she bore!"

WHAUP O' THE REDE

CANTO FIRST

CANTO FIRST

I.

THE WITCH of the cauld with a
silver comb
Sat smoothing her locks of the
tumbled foam.
On the green of the bank the primrose grew
And Spring tripped over the haughs anew
Seeking a space for her speedwell blue.
The brown trout lay at the leap o' the linn
Oaring the stream with a lazy fin;
The birch bent low with her buds of green
Till her slender form in the wave was seen;
And the dark fir whispered the secret things
He had learned from the touch of the night
wind's wings.

In the broken water the bubbles afloat
Drifted along with the freight of song
That Ettrick stole from the ousel's throat.

II.

The boughs of the hazel dipped and swung
And a boy's laugh broke where the bird had sung.
Through the parted twigs two striplings burst;
A fair haired son of the Border first;
Goodly of build and breadth was he,
Strong and straight as a pike at knee;
The fitting child of a restless hour,
 A bairn of foray and feud begot,
With the firm red mouth of the Yarrow Flower
 And the haughty brow of a Harden Scott.
Here was a lord that the March might own
When his stripling hand to the haft had grown,
And East and West might the Borders bow
To that curving lip and that constant brow.

His comrade was shaped in a slighter mould
Though his gait was as proud and his mien as bold.
He was lithe as the willow whose wands in spring
    Dance to the tune that the winds have taught her,
His hair was black as the corbie's wing,
    His dark eyes deep as the Hellmuir water.
His place seemed less by a leaguered tower
Than beside the wheel in some lady's bower.

III.

The first had a rod on his shoulder swung
    And hastened to loosen his long looped line;
From the belt of the other a light lyre hung,
    And his fingers strayed on its golden twine;
He laid him down on the river's brink
    On a mossgrown bank in the hazel shade
By the pool where the deer came down to drink,
    And, freeing his harp to his hand, he played
Taking the tune that Ettrick made:—

C

Long, long ago, ere the Yarrow wound
  Or the rainclouds filled St. Mary's,
Long, long ago, when on Ettrick ground
  The only folk were the fairies,
The breadth of the Border, parched and dried,
  Went sore from the swords of the sun,
The wild flowers drooped and the moorfowl died
  In the moss hags one by one.
Then a fairy slipped from the elfin ring
  Where her sisters danced on the Bodsbeck brae,
And wept for the woe of petal and wing
  That the sun had stolen away.

She dropped on the heath one crystal tear
  And it beamed in the bentgrass twisted,
It slid to the heart of the harebell dear,
  And it grew as the south wind kissed it.
It danced through the bracken but half revealed,
  And the Sun-god swore it should die,

But it held to his swords a silver shield
  And their blades went harmless by.
The fairy tripped by its sparkling side
  And over it held her wings,
Till it grew to a river brown and wide
  And called to the moorland things.

Then the lean red stag came down to drink
  With the fleet fawns following after;
The blackcock bathed on its silver brink
  And took home to the hills its laughter;
The wild bee came to moisten his feet
  By the spoil of the heath-flower cloyed;
The clover returned with a face more sweet
  And the daisy with new hope buoyed;
So Ettrick flowed by an elf-heart led
  With an elf-song sung the while,
And the crystal tear that a fairy shed
  Made a wasted moorland smile.

IV.

He ceased and the echoes waked and stirred
Lingering long on the tuneful word;
And his comrade, leaping the stones across,
   Weary thus soon of his fruitless ploy,
Flung himself down on the cool green moss
   And leaned with a laugh to the younger boy:
" Well did they name thee ' Whaup,' I trow,
For a very whaup o' the moor art thou
With thy wailing song and thy pinion free
And thy tender thought of the bird and bee;
But thou slightest Ettrick, O brother mine,
When thou givest us milk for his strong red wine,
And thou readest the rune of his music wrong
With a lilt of love for his raiding song.
Ah! could I but manage thy flimsy lyre
As I manage my steed on the slope of the Swire,
I would sing thee a song of my heart's desire:
Of the hungry spears that laugh in the sun
When the foray is up and the fight begun;

Of the snort of the nags as they toil at the steep;

Of the suck of the hoofs when the moss rides deep;

Of the haughty challenge; the dirl and ding,

When the pikes on the studded door plates ring,

And the long spears tremble from point to haft

With the joy of the battle!   That joy," he laughed,

" How it leaps in my blood! I have learned it all

From Gilbert and Ralph in the banquet hall

When the wine goes round and the oak logs burn

With a brighter glow for the troop's return!

And in less than a year, so my father swore,

They will have me blooded to Border war!

Ah! what is a song but meet for maids

Unless it can clang to the joy of the Raids?"

V.

At the word of challenge the younger lad

Leapt swift to his feet, but his eyes were sad,

" I know thy love of a burning beam,

    I know thy love of an empty byre,

But the joy thou seek'st is a vagrant dream,
  A will o' the wisp, and a moth's desire.
I have seen the merle, when we robbed her nest,
Haunting the hazel in hopeless quest;
I have seen the grouse, when we chased her young,
Trailing the heath with her brave heart wrung;
What of the English wife and maid
  When their slaughtered lords lie dead in the
      keep?
  When women and children are left to weep,
Tell me, brother, what joy in the raid?"

VI.

Will Scott leapt up and his eyes flashed fire
As the blood ran hot of his Border sire,
" Words for a woman!" with scorn he said,
" Is it only the English who count their dead?
Was there never a maid on Ettrick side
Who waved to her love on his last long ride?

Came never a steed over Greatmoor moss
With the corpse of his rider bound across?
For the dice deal Death as they deal renown
And the chances are square when the door goes
    down!
I am sick of this life of lilt and lyre
And the moons we waste by the Lady's fire.
I had rather the gledhawks piked mine eyne,
I had rather the corbies stripped me clean
Than I died on my couch in a curtained bower
In the ten-foot trammels of Kirkhope Tower!"

WHAUP O' THE REDE

CANTO SECOND

CANTO SECOND

I.

N THE Michaelmas moonlight,
weird and tall
The watchman stood on the peel-
tower wall,
And ever his keen eye sternly strayed
From height to haugh and from haugh to glade.
He was gloved and mailed, he was booted and
spurred,
For a Scott must ride at the lightest word,
But his head was bared to the night-wind's play
And his locks in the moon shone silver grey;
For every man between youth and age
Had ridden with Harden; and child and page,
Old man and maiden, and dame in her bower
Were the guard and the guarded in Kirkhope
Tower,

II.

The lights were low in the Lady's room
But the glow of the oak logs pierced the gloom,
And the moonlight crossing the casement white
Perched, like some pale bird out of the night,
Upon arras fold and hearthstone steel,
Upon gilded harp and spinning wheel.
On an oaken settle in poise of grief
    The Lady sat, and her broidery
Slipped from her hand as an autumn leaf
    Crumples and falls from the birchen tree.
On her pale white cheeks the tears lay wet,
    And the moonlight kissed them to mother o' pearl
As she turned to her daughter Margaret,
    Saying " Youth in its fire must be pardoned, girl!
Ay! youth must be pardoned when love or war
    Call with the spell of their witching story,
But the heart of a mother may well be sore
    When she giveth her son to the Border foray.

Your brother is nought but a child in years;
What place hath a child with the Harden spears?
Must the woman who bore him buy with tears
  What a dead man gathers of glory?"

III.

Maid Margaret sobbed in the speechless gloom,
But the sound of a light step stirred in the room
And the Whaup stood forth at the Lady's side:
"Mother, a man on the moss may ride
For a score of years, or for all his days,
And carry no mark of these farmyard frays
Save the kick of a colt or the thrust of a horn,
Or a careless knee in the oakwood torn.
Young Will o' Harden is skilled in the chase
And he knows the moor as his mother's face;
With an English loon if he crosses spear
Well—the English loon has the most to fear!"

IV.

They were kindly words, and the Lady rose

 And, taking his hand in her own white hand,

Proudly she said " His mother knows

 He will bring no shame upon Harden's band!

But what is the strength of a stripling's blows

When matched with the skill of practised foes?

Ah! would I might read by yonder star

 That wheels on the crest of dim Delorne

The gleam of the blades on Carter Bar

 Bringing me homeward my eldest born;

And would I had trooper bold to horse,

 Who have only the boys and the greybeards

  here,

I would speed him forth upon Harden's course

 To hurry me news of my youthful spear!"

" Hark to me mother!" the Whaup replied,

" I am only a stripling, but I can ride—"

She flushed at the word with a sudden dread

" Not two—not *two* of my sons!" she said,

" Shall the fawn give help when the hind's at bay?
I charge thee, Whaup, as thou lov'st me—stay! "

V.

She slipped like a wraith through the arras shroud,
As the south wind slips through a summer cloud,
And the Whaup and the maid were left alone,
And the fire burned low on the grey hearth stone.
Then the stripling bent to the weeping girl
And said " I am nought but a feckless churl,
It is little I love either helm or spur,
But our Lady—I know I would die for her
At her lightest word!   When her fingers twine
They quicken my blood like a draught of wine!
I know the track that the troop has ta'en,
I have heard it over and over again
Named by the riders at hearth and board;
I have marked in my mind each pass and ford.
Old Gilbert will lend me his gear and mail
And the moon will light me across the Ale!"

And then as she clung to his hand dismayed,
" 'Twill be one spear more to the Harden raid!
I shall win to their midst ere the fight be done,
And bring to my mother her eldest son.
At the dawn ye may tell her I served her best
By riding, myself, on my Lady's quest! "

VI.

In the mystic hush of the morning hour
Came the clatter of hoofs from Kirkhope Tower;
They crossed at the ford where Ettrick crooned
    A song to the pebbles to speed their way,
And the sorrel horse went stiff of his wound
    As he climbed the steep of the Howford brae,
But ere they had won where the wandering moon
Lit Essenside Loch with her diamond shoon
Red Rowan was galloping free on the heath
With his neck outstretched and the bit in his teeth.

VII.

'Twas a splash in the Ale where the boughs
    o'erhung,

'Twas a drag on the moor where the peat mire
    clung,

And the Whaup, who would readier walk than ride,

In his saddle was swaying from side to side;

Yet never a rein did the stripling draw

Till the stars shone red upon Ruberslaw

And he saw them again in the clear wave stir

Where the tide of Teviot splashed his spur.

As he crossed the Rule, girth deep at the ford,

A rider rose dark from the haugh and roared

With a voice that shivered the still night air

And startled the wild fowl, " Who goes there?"

" They call me the Whaup,—and 'twill serve for
    sign

That I claim my share of the moor as mine!"

D

" Bold words!" said the voice, " But thou stand'st
    confessed
No whaup but a chick from the eagle's nest,
For I know that sorrel, Wat Harden's steed,—
As who does not know him from Tyne to Tweed!
And I know that scar on his shoulder blade
For the mark of a wound my own hand made.
What errand hath brought thee to Braidhaugh
    Brow,
And where is that thief Wat Harden now?
That horse of his I have sworn to ride.
Three times when we met on the moor I tried
To wrest him from Wat o' Harden's hand,
And thrice I tasted his rider's brand,
But I swore the louder at every fall
That sorrel should one day stand in my stall.
Wilt thou yield him now?" But the Whaup
    with a frown
Drew Gilbert's gauntlet and tossed it down,
And spoke with a warrior's brave disdain
" Ye may take the steed when the rider's slain!"

VIII.

Red wrath at the heart of the reiver burned.
In the white o' the moon they wheeled and turned.
By none was the clash of their hot spears heard
Save the tod in the crags and the lone night bird.
No rules were read, no lots were drawn,
No umpire watched but the wind o' the dawn;
No marshal ordered the lonely lists
Save the marshal moon in the morning mists.
Swift in the silence the keen pikes crossed,
　　But the stranger thrust with the stouter weight,
And the battle was won and the battle lost
　　In a single leap of his lance's hate.
Stricken, the Whaup lay low on the plain
　　With a blood-red blossom beneath his knee,
And his foeman, snatching the sorrel's rein,
　　Looked down on the slight form scornfully,
While leaning forth from the morning cloud
　　The Dame of the Dawn, in splendour dressed,
Like a queen of the tourney smiled and bowed
　　And fastened her rose on the victor's breast.

IX.

Red Rob Graeme of Roughsidelea
Leading his prize rode west with glee—
" I have met Wat Harden in matches three
And thrice was the old fox match for me,
But he fashioned a gift to my eager hand
When he gave to a child his helm and brand,
And sent him forth on his saddle-tree
To shiver a lance with Roughsidelea!"

X.

The sun was high when the stripling stirred
And turned on his side with a wondering word,
Then groping in memory's mansions dim
The clash of the pikes came back to him.
He reeled to his feet, wild eyed and wan,
But the haugh was lone and his horse was gone.
Weak from his wound he staggered and sank
In a woful heap on the Rule's green bank—

" I had rather yon thief had hung me high
On a limb of the oak 'twixt earth and sky
Than left me a lingering death to die,
Waiting helpless the beak and claw
Of the carrion birds of Ruberslaw ! "

XI.

With his senses steeped in a drowsy swoon
He heard the Rule at his shoulder croon,
He heard the whirr of the grouse's wing
And the drone of a bee as it lit on the ling;
The kiss of the sun on his forehead lay
And he slept on the golden arm of the day,
While the moorland wind with its scented breath
Sweetened the far-off call of Death.
He slept and dreamed.　In a dim lit bower
That was fair as the heart of a lily flower,
Where the splendid folds of the arras clung
Like a purple cloth on an altar hung,

He lay on a silken couch at ease
  While a maiden's hands like a white dove's wings
  Fluttering over her harp's gold strings
Set the dusk athrob with its melodies.
The music ceased and the harper bowed
Low to the couch as an April cloud
Stoops to the crest of Cheviot's hill
When the skies are blue and the winds are still;
And aye as she leaned his lips above,
Round armed, beautiful, lorn for love,
She called him by name;—and the accents sweet
Were merged in the music of trampling feet.

XII.

Winding down through the steep o' the glen
With laugh and jest came the Harden men.
The noon sun glinted on rowelled heel,
On lifted lance and helm of steel;
The horses weary and splashed with foam
Stepped light on the track that led them home;

And the riders, merry as boys from school,
Spurred blythely down to the ford on Rule.
Old Wat o' Harden, tireless and keen,
Rode first of the troop; he was lithe and lean
As a Liddesdale wolf, and his glance was swift
As the glance of the sun when the low clouds lift.
Ceaseless to left and right he gazed
With his hand to his shaggy eyebrows raised,
Save now and again when he turned with pride
To the stalwart youth that rode at his side.
For young Will Scott in his first night raid
Had fitly blooded his virgin blade,
Had met the shock of an English foe
With a stout young arm and laid him low,
And the whinnying stallion a henchman led
Was the spoil of a horseman left for dead.
The haughty glance of the chief of his race
Grew soft as it fell on the boy's fair face,
And he said to himself: " In this son of mine
I have whittled a rod for the English swine;

I have bred them a ravening wolf of the wild
That shall harry their herds, in this dauntless child.
May they bow to my whelp as they've bowed to me
From the Solway sands to the grey North Sea!"

XIII.

Sudden his roving glance was stayed
By a dark form stretched in the oak tree's shade.
"Halt!" Then the bits that had jingled free
Drew tight, the lances dropped to the knee,
Each sinewy thigh on the saddle pressed
Where late the rider had lounged at rest,
For well do the tried mosstroopers know
Each rock may cover an ambushed foe.
Will Scott had reined at the word of his sire
So swift that the hoofs of his horse struck fire;
He slipped to the ground as the slight form stirred
And bent above it with wondering word,
Then he leapt to his feet with his blue eyes wide
At the stain of blood, and "The Whaup!" he cried.

Wat Harden looked down on the crimson ring,
" Tis our Whaup—and a whaup with a wounded
    wing!
What doeth this child of the chamber here
In helm and harness, with spur and spear? "
At the well known voice the stripling raised
His head, bewildered, and round him gazed
On the fretting steeds and the men in mail,
And, weak from his wound, spelt forth his tale.

XIV.

The wrath of Wat Harden was grand to see,
His spear hand trembled against his knee,
The fire in his eye could nought conceal,
And the veins on his forehead were bands of steel.
For a space no word from his pale lips passed,
Then " That was Rob Graeme! " he roared at last,
" I had rather Red Rowan lay stripped in the bog
Than he carried that reiving Liddesdale rogue!—
Bold and gentle, clever and keen,
There was never such steed on the Marches seen,

On bank and boulder, on tussock and hag,
He can change his feet like an Ettrick stag.
He has carried me fast, he has carried me far,
In revel of chase and in riot of war,
And never as yet has my lance been stayed
When the weight of my sorrel pushed home the
    blade.
He has bent to the hand of a man I trow;
Shall he bend to a thieving wastrel now?"

XV.

Then, turning fierce to his troop, he cried:—
" Ye may girth, my lads, for a longer ride;
For I take no rest and I draw no rein
Till my sorrel horse is my own again.
No cup of wine to my lips shall cling
Till red Rob Graeme lies dead on the ling!
You, Gavin and Hugh, here's work for ye both;
Bring hither an ell of that English cloth
And bind me the wound of this war-child here,
And lay him soft in your lifted gear

And bear him to Wauchope; methinks the dame
Will nurse him to health, if ye name my name!
Then haste on our tracks; ye may gather at least
Some shred of the bones where the corbies feast!"

XVI.

He spoke.   At a wave of his bridle hand
The troopers wheeled like a wildfowl band;
Swift as sleuth hounds keen on the quest
They picked up the trail where the tracks ran west,
And clattered away on the stones of the glen,
And the haugh was clear of the Harden men,
Save for Gavin and Hugh, who grumbled sore
As their burden over the ford they bore,
For the clash of blades was their only joy
And 'twas little they cared for a wounded boy.
" What aileth the old hawk?" Gavin said,
" When he flieth his chicks on an English raid?
Too soon they are free of the old bird's nest
    When they come to hamper our eager hands!

The moor is wailing with babes at breast
  And infants still in their swaddling bands!"
But they carried him up to the Wauchope wall,
And summoned the dame and told her all;
Then swung to their saddles and followed the trail
Where the sun leaned over to Liddesdale.

WHAUP O' THE REDE

CANTO THIRD

CANTO THIRD

I.

HE OAKS in the cleuch stood
golden-red,
The ripening nuts on the hazel
hung,
The purple thistle her down had sped
To the purple cloud that overhead
  Like a velvet cloak on the morning clung.
Here and there from a panel of blue
The swords of the sun struck boldly through
To pierce with a keen point, one by one,
The slender shields that the spiders spun.
Autumn had whitened the last bluebell,
With plaintive murmur the first leaves fell,

And with sigh for the oak and sob for the flower
Rule ran slowly by Wauchope Tower,
Bearing away on his throbbing breast
A leaf conferred for a love confessed.

II.

With light foot bending the golden fern
The Whaup came down by the moorland burn,
He reached for a bough of the rowan tree
   As it swung in the sunlight, scarlet and fair
With its clustered spoil, and " To-night," said he,
   " Ye shall jewel the dusk of my dear love's hair! "
Then he gathered the berries rich and red
And, bearing them home through the oakleaves
     dead,
Threaded the wood like a maid in the dance,
For the wound was healed of the raider's lance,
And light of heart and light of limb
Is a youth when his first love wakes in him.

III.

Alone in her chamber the maid Alleyne
  With white hands toiled at her tapestry,
And sang to herself some low refrain
  From the Border's martial minstrelsy;
For hers was a spirit proud and high,
And free as the Rule that hirpled by.
The heart of the Marches hot and wild
Was twin to the heart of this Border child,
And better she loved the moor's romance
Than the ploy of the bower and the swing of the
      dance.
'Twixt Esk and Till there were maidens fair
But none with the sheen of her nut-brown hair,
And none with her eyes of the hazel hue
That a heart-fire lit and a soul looked through,
Nor her rounded arm; the curve of her breast
Was a place where a warrior's head might rest;
Nor yet was the queenly Yarrow Flower
More queen than the daughter of Wauchope Tower.

E

IV.

And now like a queen she raised her head
As the stairway whispered the Whaup's light tread.
He entered and bowed with a courtly grace,
But a shadow crossed on her proud young face
As he gave her his spoils of the rowan tree
Saying " Wilt thou not wear them, fair maid, for
    me ? "

She had better loved had the oak door reeled
To the clang of some war-lord booted and steeled,
Who had challenged her joy with a joy of his own
As he gave her the spoil of some foe o'erthrown,
Or the plume of a heron his hawk had struck,
Or the antlers or hoof of a hunted buck;
She had rather had trophy of chase or war
Than the gentle gift that this stripling bore.
With some such thought her face grew grave
As she took the scarlet sprays he gave.
Though she loved him not, despite her will
She loved his song and his harping skill,

And, smiling now, to the youth she said:—
" Ye may sing me a song while I ply my thread!"
The Whaup took the great harp gently down
And, wooing his thought with a moment's frown,
Slid his slender fingers to and fro
To the words that fell with an easy flow:—

> I have given thee a rose,
>   Lady! O my Lady!
> Let thy heart around it close.
> Other hands may bring thee flowers
> Grown in richer garden-bowers,
> None so sweet as this sweet hour's,
>   Lady! O my Lady!

> Doubt and fear its thorns forbid,
>   Lady! O my Lady!
> In its heart my heart is hid.

Though its petals fold on fold
Falter in Fate's storm winds cold,
It shall keep its heart of gold,
    Lady! O my Lady!

Love's the name of my red rose,
    Lady! O my Lady!
Richer bloom no hand bestows.
Keep my rose, my Lady fair,
Guard it with a jealous care,
'Tis a flower a queen might wear,
    Lady! O my Lady!

V.

" Love, always love! " the maiden cried,
" 'Tis a paltry word in a world so wide!
Ah! If I were a Scott I would tune the strings
To a bolder note and to braver things! "
She mused for a moment, brow on hand;
" When they name thy name in the Borderland

Knight and lady and henchman bow
As they might to the name of a king, I trow!
On the golden day that they brought thee here,
Sport and spoil of a raider's spear,
I looked from my bower window down,
And I said: ' This day shall be goal and crown
Of my long desire. 'Tis a son of Wat,
And at last I shall look on a Harden Scott.
We shall nurse him to life, a man for men,
And save him to menace the March again! '
And—thou singest me paltry songs of love!
And givest for gauntlet a lady's glove! "

VI.

As the scornful words from the fair lips fell,
A flush, like the red on Yeavering Bell
When the morning sun comes out of the south,
Trembled and fluttered from brow to mouth
On the Whaup's pale face; but he spoke with fire,
" War, always war! 'Tis a poor desire!

Yet I too have heard of the joy of the raid!"
And, willing to please her, he bent and played:—

Ho! for the blades of Harden!
   Ho! for the driven kye!
The broken gate and the lances' hate
   And a banner red on the sky!
The rough road runs by the Carter;
   The white foam creams on the rein;
Ho! for the blades of Harden!
   "There will be moonlight again!"

The dark has heard them gather,
   The dawn has bowed them by,
To the guard on the roof comes the drum of a hoof
   And the drone of a hoof's reply.
There are more than birds on the hill to-night
   And more than winds on the plain!
The threat of the Scotts has filled the moss,
   "There will be moonlight again!"

Ho! for the blades of Harden!
 Ho! for the ring of steel!
The stolen steers of a hundred years
 Come home for a Kirkhope meal!
The ride must risk its fortune,
 The raid must count its slain,
The March must feed her ravens.
 " There will be moonlight again!"

Ho! for the blades of Harden!
 Ho! for the pikes that cross!
Ho! for the king of lance and ling
 —A Scott on the Ettrick moss!
The rough road runs by the Carter,
 The white foam creams on the rein;
And aye for the blades of Harden
 " There will be moonlight again!"

VII.

"Well sung! Well sung, Sir Whaup!" she cried,
"One Scott can harp if the rest can ride!
At last have I wakened the smouldering fire
That burns to betoken thee son of thy sire!"
But the Whaup stood silent, watching her face
And the rise and fall of her fingers' grace;
Then suddenly, craving a love denied,
He fell on his knee at the damsel's side:—
"Alleyne," he pleaded, with eyes a-shine,
  "There is never a song but I'd sing for thee,
  There is never a fight I would fail or flee
Were the prize a kiss from those lips of thine!
I have loved thee, sweet, since that fateful day
When with wound unstaunched on the haugh I lay,
And, cradled to sleep in the warm sunbeams,
I saw thee first in a bower of my dreams!"

VIII.

"Love, always love!" the maid replied,
"I know not what love may hold or hide,

But I know that when love my heart shall stir
He shall ride to my door with lance and spur!"
Sadly the minstrel bowed his head,
"I would I had lain in the sunshine, dead,
Ere the troopers brought me to Wauchope gate
To a second sword at the hands of Fate,
To be nursed by thy mother and thrust by thee
With a keener lance than of Roughsidelea.
To-morrow my brother to Rule doth ride
With a steed to take me to Ettrick-side,
My way lies far by the moor and fell
Wilt thou give me no hope in thy last farewell?"

IX.

Then Alleyne, with her fine scorn half forgot,
"I have told thee, Whaup, that I love thee not.
But I love thy songs, and their notes shall thrill
When thy horse's hoofs are dumb on the hill."
Then the stripling rose from his bended knee,
And loosened his brooch and his cloak set free.

He held to the maiden the clasp of gold,
A raven perched on a rampart bold,
And said " 'Tis a spoil of some foray of old
When my father rode with a raiding band
To harry the homes of Northumberland;
My mother gave it long syne to me
And I give it as token of love to thee!"
" A prize of the raid!" she cried with joy,
And stretched her hand like a child for a toy;
Then swift as a thought that hand fell free,
" I can take no token of love from thee!"
" Then take it as friendship's pledge!" said he.

X.

One moment she wavered, her eyes like stars,
While a sunbeam strayed through the casement
        bars,
Then she said " 'Tis a bird of omen ill
And of bleached white bones on a windy hill.

It has brought thee wounds, it will bring thee more,
I will take it and keep it, for *I* love war;
There is never a fate that I dare not prove
And I fear no thrust, be it lance or love!"
She spoke, and he turned and left her there
  With her splendid scorn of his love confessed,
With the rowans of Rule in her dark brown hair
  And the raven of Neville a clasp on her breast.

WHAUP O' THE REDE

CANTO FOURTH

CANTO FOURTH

I.

ILL SCOTT rode out of the
morning mist
With a hound at heel and a
hawk on his wrist,
And a henchman of Harden close in his train
With a led horse tugging the halter rein.
The storm in the night had twisted the fern,
And the rain had flooded the Wauchope burn.
The black horse snorted and wheeled at the ford
But Will sat straight as a handed sword,
And striking his spur in the stallion's flank
Made him face the flood and the further bank.
Lightly Alleyne stepped forth from her bower,
Fresh as a wild wet woodland flower;

She heard a voice to the courtyard call
And climbed the stair to the rampart wall,
And there as she looked where the riders passed
Came a light to her eyes, for it seemed at last
She had found in the form of this stalwart squire
The lord of her dreams and her long desire.
The foam-flecked steeds were left in stall,
    The hound was kennelled, the hawk was fed,
The spurs rose ringing from court to hall,
    And the Whaup and Will their welcomes said.
Then the Whaup, " What news hast thou brought
        for me?
And what of Red Rowan and Roughsidelea? "

II.

All Rule Water, east and west,
    Bowed to the spell of Turnbull's name,
And among the proud of the Borders' best
    There was none so proud as the Wauchope dame.
And now as she sat at her daughter's side
    While the heir of Harden told his tale

'Twas the throb of a raider's heart of pride
  Beat time to the hoofs through Liddesdale!
And Alleyne, with her soft dark eyes grown bold,
Let them feast on his lips for the tale they told.

III.

" 'Twas a reckless gallop," Will Harden said,
" Through the boulders tall and the burn's rough
        bed,
Thrice was my spur in the soft mire set,
And thrice my girths and the grey moss met,
But my father slackened no whit in the chase
As he pressed his mare to her topmost pace.
The westering sun on his mailed hand shone
As he stood in his stirrups and waved us on.
Sudden we saw on the face of the steep
Our hunted quarry like foxes creep;
The nag of the reiver was well nigh spent,
With a dragging hoof and his nose to the bent,
And old Red Rowan, a lather of foam,
Went slugging and sullen with head from home.

F

Then my father turned to his reckless troop

  As he drove at the hill with spur and hand,

And roared ' Let the Eskdale eagles stoop,

  And the corbies gather from Cumberland!'

I saw the thief in his saddle turn,

And leap to his feet with his back to the burn;

Then the eager troop like a torrent burst

In one whelming wave—but old Wat was first!"

IV.

The Lady rose right haughtily,

" So perish," she cried, " such curs as he!"

And Alleyne sat dumb with her lips apart

And a heaving bosom and beating heart,

For the blood of her forbears leapt and stirred

At the picture drawn in a careless word.

Then Will to the Whaup: " The days grow short,

We have far to ride and the moor holds sport;

I trust that my hawk has been lightly fed,

It is time for the hood to be over her head

And the horses brought and thy farewells said!"

They rode from the court, and Alleyne looked down
  And waved her scarf from the rampart stair,
For the Whaup she had only a careless frown
  But she kissed her hand to Harden's heir.

V.

As they rose the hill to the north of Rule
A heron flapped from a lonely pool.
Into the wind Will tossed his hawk
Like a brown leaf whirled from the myrtle stalk.
Swiftly she climbed in circling flight
Till she seemed a speck on the cloud bank white,
Then launched like a dart on her downward way
And bore to the heath her helpless prey.
Will sprang from his horse with a hunter's pride
And " A kill, and a right good kill! " he cried,
" Now if I had a maid like that maid of thine
  With the soft dark eyes in Wauchope Tower,
I would shear her a plume, O minstrel mine,
  For a trophy to hang on the wall of her bower."

The brow of the Whaup flushed suddenly red,
" Keep to thy hawk and thy hound!" he said,
" When the daughter of Wauchope needs thy boon
She will doubtless tell thee, and that right soon!"
Will Scott had bent as he blooded his bird
But he leapt to his feet at the passionate word,
" Ho! Ho!" he laughed, " my cock o' the wild,
Hast thou lost thy heart to that wan-faced child?"
The Whaup rode on in silent scorn
But the rift was made and the quarrel born.

VI.

The sun was low when they crossed the Ale,
It was dark when they won to Ettrick vale,
And the stars on Singlie had blazed an hour
When the watchman challenged on Kirkhope
          Tower.
The hall was lit, the board was spread;
Walter of Harden sat, stern, at the head.
As their spurs on the threshold struck with a clang
" The Whaup! The Whaup!" to the rafters rang.

One asked for his wound, while three in a breath
Told over the tale of his foeman's death,
And Harden said " Thou hast tried thy wings
And hast learned how a Liddesdale lance-point
    stings.
Henceforth thou shalt lay thine harp aside
And ride with my troop when next I ride! "

VII.

From hand to hand the wine-cup passed
    And Will from the flagon drank full and free
Till his face grew flushed, and turning at last
    With a bantering blow on the dour Whaup's knee,
He cried, till the furthest page could hear
    And listening paused with his wine cup stayed:
" Ay, the Whaup has learned from a Liddesdale
        spear,
    But more, I ween, from a Wauchope maid!"
A smile rode rippling from face to face,
    The troopers roared and the pages grinned;

The angry Whaup rose hot in his place
  While round him the laughter reeled and dinned,
And lifting his cup ere a man could rise
He dashed it full in Will Harden's eyes.
'Twas heftily hurled, 'twas aimed right well,
  And as victim falls to the foeman's sword
With scarcely a groan the stripling fell
  Twixt the steel-hung wall and the banquet board.

VIII.

Like a skep of bees when a stone is hurled,
  Like a rabbit warren when footsteps sound,
In a moment the great hall seethed and swirled
  As trooper and varlet crowded round.
From his seat at the board, dark-browed and grim,
Wat rose and the vassals made way for him.
" Stand back ! " he roared—they were swept aside,
For they bowed to that voice in revel or ride.
He raised his son with his strong right arm,
While blood on his hand dropped crimson and warm,
Then his wrath broke forth like a bursting storm.

And the Whaup stood cowering, white to the lips,
'Neath the scorn of the words that scourged like whips:
" A coward trick, and an English blow!
As the cur is bred, so the whelp will grow!
Little I thought when we brought thee here
A puling babe in its swaddling gear,
Thou would'st ravening turn on the hand that fed!
Is thy debt already so far forgot
That thou liftest thine arm to a Harden Scott?"

IX.

In the trembling hush the sob of a page
Flung fuel afresh upon Harden's rage:
" A foundling whelp that to humour a whim
I saved from the fate set down for him!
Had I known this cub of the South had teeth
I had drawn my dirk from its dangling sheath
And driven it home on the Carter heath;
    'Twould better have suited the English swine
Than to let him shelter this roof beneath,
    And a Neville darken a door of mine!"

Then he called to a trooper standing by,
Saying " Rope me the dastard and hang him high!
Let the crows a meal on his carcase make!"
Then suddenly: " Nay! for my Lady's sake
I will spare his life. Let him sink or swim,
    Let him wander homeless on hill or plain.
Fling him forth and his false harp after him,
    So I never look on his face again!"

X.

The Whaup in silence bowed his head,
No hand he raised, no word he said
While he trod with Ralph the winding stair
As one who knows that his doom is fair.
But when his warder had loosed the bars
And they stood in the cold white scorn of the stars
He turned to the trooper and gently sought
The truth of the tale that this hour had brought.
" Ay!" said Ralph Scott, " I remember well
Yon windy knowe on the Carter Fell,

When thy tiny wail from the blankets broke
And the old hawk turned at the sound and spoke,
" Ho! Ralph! hast thou harried some grey-hen's
    nest?''
And I searched in the silks. And the Neville crest
Was agleam on the bands that bound thy breast.
It was I that carried thee home from Rede,
And I know thee a Neville of Ravensmead!''
The Whaup stood white in the white starshine,
  With his kerchief held in a last behest,
Saying: " Give to the Lady this scarf of mine
  From the son of her sons that loved her best!''
Then he took his harp from the trooper's hand
And, a shadow, faded in shadowland.

WHAUP O' THE REDE

CANTO FIFTH

CANTO FIFTH

I.

OME ELF of the clouds had witched
the night,
And the morning woke to a world
of white.
Crest and hollow were drifted deep,
Between them the glidders stood black and steep,
And on every heath on the hillside set
The snow had woven a coverlet.
The sun was high; the wind of the morn
Shook a silver dust from the frosted thorn,
And drove the clouds on the heights apart,
Laying bare the blue to the Border's heart.
The twisted pines that fretted the sky
Waved snow-white flags as the breeze went by,

And Yarrow lay dark at Whitehope's feet
Like a warrior's blade on his winding sheet.

II.

A lone wayfarer trudged in the snow
Where the rough path ran by the river's flow;
No trail could be seen in haugh or glade
Save the winding track that his footprints made;
No sound could be heard in hope or glen
To tell that his world was a world of men.
He was young and strong, but his step was slow
Like the step of a wanderer loth to go,
And aye he turned where the river bends,
    And waved to the hills he loved and knew,
As a man may turn to his watching friends
    And wave farewell ere they fade from view.
And once he stood, while his harp, unslung,
Its notes o'er the snow-white silence flung.

III.

O leaden river trailing
   Through winter's kingdom grey,
While winds of winter wailing
   Blow down thy lonely way,
In thought I see thee sailing
   Across the summer day.

I see the white clouds hover
   Above Blackandro's crest;
I see the heath-bush cover
   The grey-hen's simple nest.
Once more I walk, thy lover,
   Beside thy silver breast.

I hear the brown burns singing
   Old songs of hope and joy,
From out the hill tops bringing
   The peace no years destroy.
I see the wild flowers springing
   I gathered as a boy.

O steel-blue streamlet bearing
  Old memories deep and dear!
O snow white mountains wearing
  The grave-sheets of the year!
Farewell! my feet go faring,
  My heart, my heart, stays here!

IV.

Thus the minstrel sang of departed days,
  Then gently sighing, he turned his face
From the Yarrow Vale and the well-known ways
  That fate had forbidden his feet retrace;
And sudden he saw at his shoulder stand
The walls of Newark, grey towered and grand.
The scarpments glittered, a silver sheath
Hiding the sword of the strength beneath,
And high on the western rampart flew
The Border flag of the Bold Buccleuch.
Beneath it the stranger well might pause
  And the breadth and power of its purpose scan,

For higher than King and Kirk and Laws
  That banner had power to bless or ban.
But the wanderer, weary of pomp and pride,
Dreamed only of love as he passed beside,
And threaded his way through the oakwood brown
To the diamond roofs of Selkirk town.

V.

Where Yarrow and Ettrick mingling met
  Tweed water brown with the melted snow,
He bade farewell with a fond regret
  To the streams of his youth and their friendly flow,
And brighter the flame of his purpose burned
As his heart found strength and his hope returned.
His sad dark eyes and his wistful face
Won pity and favour from place to place,
Nor sought he for food or shelter long
Who could pay for the gift with such gift of song!
The Abbot of Melrose wished him speed,
  The monks of Dryburgh blessed his way,

G

He stole a lilt from the lips of Tweed
  And harped in their halls his debt to pay;
And at Norham Castle he cried " I stand
A Neville at last in Northumberland! "

VI.

To him whose patriot pride is stirred
  By memories of the past revealed,
Though long resigned to fox and bird
  What spot so sad as Flodden Field!
Where each green slope and every glade
Resounds with clash of helm and blade;
Where round the rough crest every rood
Is watered by some Scotsman's blood!

VII.

The minstrel climbed the sacred mound
  And gazing eastward where the Till
To Tweed his devious pathway wound
  Through woods that fringed that fatal hill,

Unbound his harp and thus deplored
The strife his gentle soul abhorred:—

    O warriors in your trenches laid
      To sleep away God's golden hours
    Where rusted helm and broken blade
      Deck all this fateful hill for flowers,
    What worth is there in victory
    When best and worst lie knee to knee?

    Say, what avails the lusty blow,
      The good shaft driven till it jars,
    When in the dark ye no more know
      The rise and set of sun and stars?
    What fenceth victory from defeat
    When over both the fern leaves meet?

    What boots it now that Till ran blood,
      Or Tweed flowed salt with Scotland's tears?
    'Twould take than Till a broader flood
      To clean your purpled Flodden spears!

Not all the snow on Millfield Plain
Could make those white blades white again!

Not all the silence of the grave
  Can hush this hill where horror trod,
Or still the death-cry of the brave
  Swept suddenly to face their God!—
Hark! Muffled hoofs! Dead horsemen
    steeled
Ride slow, ride slow, round Flodden Field!

VIII.

This song, lone hill and leafless tree
Gave back with plaintive melody,
While round the harper circling sped
The restless spirits of the dead.
With whisper of their wings for wage
The youth resumed his pilgrimage,
And crossing Millfield's marshy plain
Held south, and so turned west again

Till Yeavering Bell behind him lay
And Hethpool's glen and Cheviot grey,
While Rede grew nearer day by day.
By friendly farm and wayside inn
    He passed, and oft, when red and bright
The crackling oak logs blazed within,
    Or when some streaming window light
Across his lonely pathway poured,
    He shared full many a jovial night
And tuned his harp to cheer the board.

IX.

As Spring approached, the minstrel's heart
    Grew glad with the murmur of homing wings,
For the sweetest note of the harper's art
    Is the song of love that the Springtide brings,
And under a blue sky flecked with cloud
The wanderer sang with a love-note loud.
As the silvery echoes trembled and died,
A sudden voice at his shoulder cried:—

" Well sung, Sir Knight!" and there stood alone
On the wide grey moor an agèd crone.

X.

Her cheek was brown as the winter heath,
　Her eyes were dark as the blackthorn bough,
Like fangs of the wolf were her yellow teeth,
　And the lines lay raggèd across her brow
　Like the furrows scored by a careless plough.
Her hand was crooked like the eagle's claw
　That clings to the Cheviot cliff-top rude,
As of one who lives by the moorland's law
　And tears at the moorland's bones for food.
" What is thine errand, Sir Knight?" she croaked,
" That thou roamest the fells thus minstrel-cloaked?
Do kings' sons harp to the moorland birds?
Do princes tramp on the heath like herds?"
But the youth replied with his gentle grace
" No prince am I, and of no king's race,
But I am a Neville, and all my need
Is to find my mother and Ravensmead."

XI.

The crone looked East, and the crone looked West,
" 'Tis an easy word, but an empty quest.—
'Tis twenty years since the tower ye name
Went down to the wold in smoke and flame.
'Tis twenty years since the Lady fled
From the wasted home where her lord lay dead.
Turn ye to Tyne!" The minstrel heard,
And bowed his head to the hopeless word.
But the gipsy smiled on him " Turn to Tyne,
For there what thou lovest in life is thine!"
A trembling joy in his dark eyes shone,
He turned with a word—but the witch was gone.
A moment he pondered, in doubt distressed,
With a lingering glance to the golden west,
Then seeking the south that held his shrine,
Heard the low hills echo " To Tyne! To Tyne!"

WHAUP O' THE REDE

CANTO SIXTH

CANTO SIXTH

I.

NIGHT wrapped the Rule in a
purple pall
But the logs were blazing in
Wauchope hall.
A pedlar, fresh from the Tweedside fairs,
Displayed to the vassals his trinket wares,
And won scant custom; but won renown
By relating the gossip of tower and town.
He told a tale that was common word
With the Yarrow laird and the Ettrick herd,
How a son of the Scotts had proved to be
A foundling out of the South country,
A Neville brought from the English side
In the bundled spoil of a Harden ride.

He told a tale of a drunken brawl
When hot words passed in the Kirkhope hall;
How Wat of Harden in anger wild
Had flung from the doors his foster-child;
How the Lady of Kirkhope was stricken with woe;
How the Laird had forgiven the hasty blow,
But the youth and his harp had fled from ken—
On the road to the Rede, thought the Harden men!
This garrulous tale a handmaid heard
And brought to her mistress word by word.

II.

Alleyne, since the well remembered day
When the youths of Kirkhope had ridden away,
Had pined and fretted for sake of one
She had thought the while to be Harden's son,
For she learned from her maiden heart ere long
That her love was bound to a lyre and song,
That no warrior steeled and no hunting squire,
But this minstrel youth, was her dear desire.

She heard his harp on the windy hill,
She heard his voice when the nights were still.
She remembered the tender charm of his face
His courtly mien and his lissome grace,
And knew by her virgin bosom's stir
There was no other lord in life for her.

III.

When Mirren the maid her tale had told
Alleyne took forth from her mantle's fold
The raven clasp she had oft caressed,
And long she gazed on the Neville crest.
" Neville or Scott," she sobbed at last
While her tears on the golden brooch fell fast,
" He wanders alone on the ambushed lea,
Belike no mail and no horse hath he.
The moor is blue with a hundred blades,
And his road is the road of the English raids.
Ah! why did I speed him to Harden's hate,
To the open wold and the spears of Fate?"

But the lairds of Rule had been brave to dare,
And their spirit was strong in this damsel fair,
To Mirren she whispered her dauntless plan:
She would be master, her maid be man;
They would don the trappings of knight and page
And ride to the Rede in pilgrimage.
The horses were borrowed, the gear bespoke,
　The secret was kept from the Lady's ear,
And they rode from the tower ere morning broke,
　With helm and harness and lifted spear.

IV.

They rode for a day and they rode for two,
　In heath and bracken, by scaur and burn,
Till they won to the vale that Rede runs through
　With many a silver twist and turn.
Reeling, weary and travel stained,
The Byrness lands they had scarcely gained,
Ere a witch-like form rose out of the moss
And cried as it halted their path across:

" What wilful errand hath brought ye here,
O masking maids, in mosstrooping gear?
Do rounded arms cross swords with men?
Do white hands gather the gifts o' the glen? "
Then answered Alleyne right haughtily
" And what is our errand to such as thee?—
Yet, maybe thou knowest this land of Rede
And a road by the moor to Ravensmead?"

V.

With her bird-like hand on the maiden's cloak
The old wife laughed as the ravens croak,
Then parted her thin brown lips and spoke—
" The tower that ye seek stands no more here,
'Twas a long line's pyre and a brave man's bier
And its walls are level this twenty year.
Turn ye to Tyne!"   Alleyne as she heard
Gave a sudden cry at the hopeless word,
But the old crone smiled on her, " Turn to Tyne,
And all that thou lovest in life is thine!"

WHAUP O' THE REDE

CANTO SEVENTH

H

CANTO SEVENTH

I.

N A GOLDEN garden bright with
    flowers
  A lady walked through the
    morning hours
Seeking the buds that the sun had sent
And tying the stalks that the rain had bent.
Her hair was white as the upland snow,
  And deep in the heart of her liquid eyes
Lay the leaden weight of some ancient woe
  As a boulder dark in a deep pool lies.
Where close in their caves on an oaken board
Her bees still clung to their winter hoard
She paused and listened, then bending near
She crooned this song to her pages dear.

Wake, little bees; the sun is shining,
  The daisies are come and the oak buds break;
The thorn's in bloom and the vetch is twining—
    Wake, little brown bees,
      Wake!

Go, little bees; the speedwell glistens,
  The gorse is out in a golden row;
The lark is in song and the whole world listens,
    Go, little brown bees,
      Go!

Fly, little bees; in your brave disorder;
  Serried and single, low and high;
Bear me a message beyond the Border,
    Fly, little brown bees,
      Fly!

Speed, little bees; my love-word taking;
  He that I love shall hear and heed;

Tell him my heart is breaking, breaking—

   Speed, little brown bees,

      Speed!

II.

As though in answer one lone bee flew

By her shoulder north, and was lost in the blue.

As the Lady followed its winding flight

She saw on the hill a mail-clad knight;

She watched him rein by the farmstead wall

And heard him turn to his page and call

A stern command that he voice their needs

Of rest for themselves and their weary steeds.

As she loitered still in the lavender

She heard a step on the lawn-grass stir

And turned, and the knight stood close to her.

An old hope leaped to life in her breast

"Ye are come from the North?"   Then the Neville

   crest

Blazed in the sun. With a sudden joy
She cried, "Ye have news of my baby boy!
For that was the brooch these mother hands
Fastened for clasp on his kirtle bands
On that direful day when the red flames leapt,
And my warrior fought and my baby slept.
Ye have news of my son, for that brooch ye bear
Should none but the friend of a Neville wear!"

III.

And Alleyne replied, while her wonder grew,
"Ah! Lady his mother, I love him too!
He gave me for token this clasp of gold
As a clasp my heart to his heart to hold.
I have ridden the moor from Rule to Rede,
To search for his castle of Ravensmead;
I have ridden the fells from Rede to Tyne
To give myself to this lord of mine.
For I am no Border knight or squire
But a maiden seeking her heart's desire."

Then she lifted her helm. 'Twas a maid stood there,
And the wind was full of her blown brown hair.
In a common grief their eyes grew wet,
In a new-born hope their mute lips met.
From noon to night in the lady's bower
They tarried with locked hands, hour by hour,
Till the moonlight wandered the casement through
To list to the love tale told anew.

IV.

Even love at last had no more to tell
And a hush on the moonlit chamber fell,
Till the wail of a harp 'neath the window played
Woke wistful mother and weary maid.
One moment stood, as the sweet notes swelled,
Alleyne, by the music witched and spelled,
Then swift as a startled woodland bird
Which a step in the autumn leaves has stirred
She flew to the ground by the turret stair
With the moonbeams wreathed in her unbound hair,

And cleaving the song with her cry of love

Felt the strong arms binding her arms above.

. . . . So havened at last in that Tyneside

    bower

Three hearts found love's enchanted hour.

V.

On the joy of the meeting a frighted maid

Burst suddenly, wailing " A raid!   A raid!"

Scarce had the Whaup leapt bold to his feet

When he heard the hoofs in the pasture beat.

He looked from the window and saw them pass,

A stalwart troop in the Tyneside grass,

And first of them all was a form he knew

Broad of shoulder, with eyes of blue.

Then the Whaup his scarf from the casement flew.

A spurred heel rang on the winding stair,

And a curtain swung, and Will Scott stood there.

VI.

He looked on the Whaup and their fingers twined;
He looked on Alleyne and his eyes were kind;
He looked on the Lady and swift he guessed
Of an ancient grief that had found its rest.
Then he turned again to the Whaup and said—
" I knew thee lost and I thought thee dead;
Brother I searched for thee far and near
And now in thy joy I find thee here!
Wilt thou pardon my scornful words to thee
As I pardon the blow thou gavest me?
Forgive my father!   Forget thy wrongs!
Come back to Scotland and make her songs!"

VII.

Then taking the hand Will Harden gave,
The Whaup replied in accents grave—
" Thy father smote us with sword and flame,
   He drove our cattle, he slew my sire,

He took from the Nevilles their ancient name

   To tread it with scorn in the Marches' mire;

But thy lady mother—may God be good

For her noble sake to all womanhood!—

Unwrought the wrong of Wat Harden's hate

With her love that led me to man's estate,

And because for this hour she has let me live

I can look on a Scott and can still forgive!"

Will Scott looked down with a flush of shame,

Then he bent his knee to the grief-worn dame—

"*Thy* pardon, too, wilt thou let me take?"

And, weeping, she said, "For thy mother's sake."

VIII.

Then Will to his feet leapt sudden and soon,

"My horses are fretting with heads to the moon.

I can hear the low of the waiting kine,

And the dawn must find us afar from Tyne!"

He turned, and his step on the stairway rang;

Through the open door came the courtyard clang.

He lifted his horn to his lips and blew;
The ready fingers the reins ran through;
The saddles were filled, the steeds advanced
And neighed to the night till their bit-rings danced;
And those that watched from the casement bars
Caught the tossing white of the forehead-stars,
Saw the moonlight gleam on the burnished steel,
Saw the troop at the word of their leader wheel,
And the horses fade as they faced the glen,
And the shadows gather the Harden men.

NOTES

———

THE following short Notes have been added at the request of the publisher for the benefit of those readers who are as yet unacquainted with the district in which the scenes of the ballad are laid. For the many who know the Border, or who are familiar with its History and Literature, they are, of course, unnecessary.

REDE.—A River in Northumberland, running through a rich pastoral valley much favoured ot the raiders on account of the fat stock always to be found therein.

WAT HARDEN.—Walter Scott of Harden, known generally as **Auld Wat o' Harden.** One of the most famous of the Border Reivers. He died in 1629.

KIRKHOPE TOWER.—A famous Border fortress, the walls of which may still be seen near the village of Ettrick Bridge End, eight miles above Selkirk. The tower belonged to the Scotts of Harden, and was for a time their residence.

THE YARROW FLOWER.—Wife of Walter Scott of Harden, and daughter of Philip Scott of Dryhope. Known far and wide as the Flower of Yarrow, and noted for her wonderful beauty.

HELLMUIR WATER.—Hellmuir is a loch near the head of the Ale, distinguished for its great depth and the darkness of its waters.

ST. MARY'S.—The well-known St. Mary's Loch, goal and shrine of Yarrow's many thousand visitors.

GREATMOOR.—A considerable hill in the Hawick district.

YEAVERING BELL.—A hill at the East end of the Cheviot range.

DELORNE.—The local name for Deloraine. A hill in Ettrick.

"THERE WILL BE MOONLIGHT AGAIN."—"Reparabit cornua Phoebe," the motto of the Scotts of Harden. An allusion to the fact that they may be looked for to begin their raids afresh as each moon appears.

TURNBULL'S NAME. — The Turnbulls formed by far the most powerful clan on Rule Water and one of the most noted and feared upon the Border.

WHITEHOPE.—A hill in Yarrow.

BLACKANDRO.—A hill in the lower reaches of Yarrow.

WILL SCOTT.—Eldest son of Wat o' Harden and the Flower of Yarrow. Afterwards became Sir William Scott, married Muckle-Mou'ed Meg under romantic circumstances, and had three sons and five daughters.

SINGLIE.—A hill in Ettrick.

NEWARK.—Newark Tower, a fortress of great strength and commanding position. Its walls still stand on Yarrow.

FRASER,
ASHER,
& CO. LTD
PRINTERS

164 HOWARD ST
◆ GLASGOW ◆